Fear Of Intimacy

The Ultimate Guide To Overcome Fear Of Intimacy For Life

James Scott

Table of Contents

Introduction

Chapter 1. Intimacy: Wanting it vs. Fearing it

Chapter 2. The Two Other Fears Underlying Intimacy Anxiety: Rejection And Engulfment

Chapter 3. Up-Close With Fear Of Intimacy Anxiety: Causes, Signs And Symptoms

Chapter 4. Tips To Overcome Your Fear Of Intimacy

Conclusion

Introduction

I want to thank you and congratulate you for purchasing the book, *"Fear Of Intimacy: The Ultimate Guide To Overcome Fear Of Intimacy For Life"*.

This book contains proven steps and strategies on how to overcome your fear of intimacy, also called as intimacy anxiety. The signs and symptoms that will help you or your partner overcome this fear are also presented in this book. You will also learn about other factors that intensify the fear.

Emotional intimacy is one of the most fulfilling things anyone can experience. It makes you feel needed and important. Having intimacy makes you feel like you're not alone in this world and that you can share your whole self – your passion, dreams, thoughts, and your creativity with another human being. However, despite the positive feelings that intimacy can provide, there are still some that fear it.

Have you ever been in a relationship that's totally amazing and harmonious, and yet suddenly, you feel like you want some space or distance from your partner? Have you ever felt like being afraid of opening yourself up to others or even to your friends? These things are signs that you have fear of being intimate with other people, be that an intimate partner, a friend, or even family members.

Some people have been in relationships they really care about but the relationship is doomed to fail because of such fears. Some people truly love someone but end up hurting those people closest to them. Fear of intimacy must be dealt with. Identifying the problem, knowing what signs and symptoms there are, and facing it will help you in your journey to overcome this kind of fear.

If you are tired of failed relationships rooted from seemingly unexplainable behavior, the need to distance yourself, being afraid of sharing your thoughts with others, and bad communication, this book offers a clear and simple explanation of the issue.

The goal of this book is for you to identify the real problem. You'll know about other issues that magnify this fear and the important steps you can undertake to overcome it.

Thanks again for purchasing this book. I hope you enjoy it!

☐ **Copyright 2014 by James Scott - All rights reserved.**

This document is geared towards providing exact and reliable information in regards to the topic and issue covered. The publication is sold with the idea that the publisher is not required to render accounting, officially permitted, or otherwise, qualified services. If advice is necessary, legal or professional, a practiced individual in the profession should be ordered.

- From a Declaration of Principles which was accepted and approved equally by a Committee of the American Bar Association and a Committee of Publishers and Associations.

In no way is it legal to reproduce, duplicate, or transmit any part of this document in either electronic means or in printed format. Recording of this publication is strictly prohibited and any storage of this document is not allowed unless with written permission from the publisher. All rights reserved.

The information provided herein is stated to be truthful and consistent, in that any liability, in terms of inattention or otherwise, by any usage or abuse of any policies, processes, or directions contained within is the solitary and utter responsibility of the recipient reader. Under no circumstances will any legal responsibility or blame be held against the publisher for any reparation, damages, or monetary loss due to the information herein, either directly or indirectly.

Respective authors own all copyrights not held by the publisher.

The information herein is offered for informational purposes solely, and is universal as so. The presentation of the information is without contract or any type of guarantee assurance.

The trademarks that are used are without any consent, and the publication of the trademark is without permission or backing by the trademark owner. All trademarks and brands within this book are for clarifying purposes only and are the owned by the owners themselves, not affiliated with this document.

Chapter 1. Intimacy: Wanting it vs. Fearing it

Almost everyone wants intimacy. We want someone to share their thoughts with. They want someone to trust, to love, and to laugh with. We want someone they can share their lives with.

But the thing is, a number of us are afraid of intimacy. This is because intimacy also means that you have to open yourself up to the other person- be it a friend or a lover.

It means letting yourself be vulnerable and standing naked in front of the criticizing eyes of others. It means letting your guards down. And people, by nature, are afraid of letting their defenses down. It is a normal mechanism for humans - to guard themselves always and not to allow people to find something that might be used against them. It is a part of the survival instinct of humans, which is why some of us are extremely cautious to be intimate with others.

So, what really is fear of intimacy?

Fear of intimacy is considered as a type of anxiety wherein a person suffering it is extremely afraid of emotional closeness or getting attached to another person. The fear of being sexually intimate with a romantic partner can also arise out of this fear. If you fear being intimate with someone, you are reluctant to open up and be genuine for the fear that you will be rejected for exposing your real self.

The fear of intimacy is a generally unconscious process, but you can observe its effect on your behavior especially when you are in a relationship. You'll see it when you shove away your lover, friend, or a family member who's trying to get close to you. You'll see it when you are non-reactive to their fondness or other acts of showing love. It is obvious when you suppress the positive qualities your partner finds lovable, thereby making yourself less desirable. Those behaviors help to reduce your anxiety, preserve your negative self-image and ultimately maintain your psychological balance. It keeps you stable in your comfort zone.

In addition, you might fear intimacy because it brings you close to someone you don't know. Simply put, you open up yourself to a complete stranger. Completely opening up to someone is the only way for intimacy to come in. And the sad thing is, most people are afraid of letting down their defenses because it means letting people see them behind the mask; it's like opening your closet for people to see and judge. You will find yourself asking the following questions: *Who knows what they will think or say upon seeing the real you? Who knows what they'll do with your weak points, with your imperfections, with your frailties and vulnerability.* That's what people are afraid of. But the conflict comes in because people also want intimacy.

As much as people fear intimacy, it's also with that same magnitude that they long for it. People want to be needed and want to be heard because otherwise, life would be a lonesome boring journey. However, fulfilling a certain level of intimacy requires a really huge step and some people just can't do that. They just can't open up themselves and risk getting hurt. And in most cases, people are not just afraid of what others will see but they're also afraid of having to deal with opening old wounds. It's like facing their mistakes again and feeling all those negative emotions again. Most people just can't afford to face these emotions the second time around.

So, if you come to think of it. If you really dig deeper into the fear of intimacy, you'll realize that there are other things that intensify this fear.

Is it really intimacy that people fear? If it makes someone feel needed, loved, and treasured, then why most people choose to run away from being intimate with someone? Why most people don't dare to open up themselves to others?

Psychologists have come to realize that people do not entirely fear just intimacy. It is not intimacy that they fear but the other things that come along with it. These things are the other fears that intensify the fear of intimacy. Other people don't want to open up themselves because they fear that people might not like what they will see. And, along with this fear is having that fear of losing control or losing themselves in the process. These two fears are the fear of rejection and fear of engulfment. These two magnify the fear of intimacy.

Chapter 2. The Two Other Fears Underlying Intimacy Anxiety: Rejection And Engulfment

Having an intimate relationship with someone means having an open relationship with them. It means that you can be together and can talk about anything under the sun. It means laughing at the most stupid things around and just being crazy together. Intimacy can open a more carefree and lighter world for both you and your partner. It fills out the emptiness inside you.

If this is the case, why do most people choose to back out or run away when they feel too close to someone?

As stated in the previous chapter, psychologists found that most people with the fear of intimacy are not entirely afraid with the thought of being close to someone. It's actually the fear of being rejected when the other person finds out what's hidden inside their closet. It's also about having the fear of losing themselves in the process or getting overwhelmed with the feeling and then end up getting hurt.

During your childhood days, you may have encountered a lot of things that have triggered these fears. Some people might have felt so loved and cared during their early years, which resulted to experiences that are more positive in the future. Others have experienced being abandoned, forgotten, hurt, abused, or bullied which also contributed to how they react today. These experiences from the childhood days of a person can affect his or her perception of intimacy.

When you haven't dealt your past emotional experiences, especially the painful ones, there are tendencies that you just keep all those baggage inside you. The baggage stays with you. Therefore, there will be times that when you're hurt, you withdraw yourself from others just for the sake of avoiding getting hurt again. This is especially true for those people who have been in a relationship that they truly cared about but they ended up getting hurt. Unless these issues are addressed and faced, they will continue to pile up and will cause you to fear facing the same things again and having to deal with the same painful emotion again.

Fear of Rejection

Everyone wants to love and be loved. You might want to find a loving partner who will take care of you and be together until you grow old. You might have been fantasizing for that person who can spend the rest of your life with without having the feeling of getting tired of each other's presence. These thoughts are okay but know that true love is not as easy in reality. A lasting relationship and true love can be only be achieved when a substantial level of intimacy has been reached. But the experience of intimacy often threatens people's self-defense. It arouses the anxiety of feeling exposed and getting rejected in the end thus making intimacy a fearsome experience.

The fear of rejection is the feeling of fear of being not accepted. It's also the feeling of losing someone you love or care. For this very reason, many people shy away from fulfilling relationships. They shy away from intimacy and from showing their true colors to others thinking that the other person might not like what they will see and go away. So, instead of waiting for someone to leave them or reject them then get the feeling of being left behind, they pull away first from others and stay in their comfort zone where they feel protected and safe.

This fear of being rejected sprouted during the developmental years. These are the times when things are changing inside the body and the environment as well. When you experienced a substantial level of pain out of rejection, you fear of being hurt thus making you reluctant to take on another relationship again.

These negative feelings develop and pile up which becomes a part of who you think you are as a person. Simply put, those feelings affect your perception about things and your self-image. So, when someone shows interest in you and gets closer to you, you experience an internal war between their view of you and your own self-image. You then, react with doubt and suspicion because you fear that when intimacy levels up and you begin to open up yourself, people might shy away from you when they know your real story.

Fear of engulfment

Aside from the fear of rejection, the fear of engulfment is another major factor that magnifies the fear of intimacy. Some people are afraid of intimacy because they don't like the feeling of losing control over a situation. When the intimacy levels up, there is a tendency that some people may lose grip of themselves and that the overwhelming feeling brought about by intimacy will consume them. This thought or perception about intimacy makes people afraid of going to the next level, to being intimate with someone.

Humans are known for having a higher intelligence and their thought process is more complex than of other mammals on earth. This is also the reason why one of the fears of many people is the fear of not knowing. When someone is consumed by something, one cannot know what happens next or where it would lead. Usually, this fear of losing control and having no ability to control oneself is the reason why other people do not want to get intimate.

These two factors play a huge role in answering the most obvious and deeper questions regarding the fear of intimacy. Why are some people afraid of rejection? Why others don't know how to handle with such situations and why do they take rejection personally? These questions will always be around when you try to deal with intimacy anxiety. And the only way to get rid of these questions is to deal with them one by one.

Chapter 3. Up-Close With Fear Of Intimacy Anxiety: Causes, Signs And Symptoms

In every kind of emotional or mental issue, the first step is always determining the root cause of the problem. You can never solve an issue if you don't even know what to solve. So, in order to put a stop on your fear of intimacy, you must first determine why you have this fear and the signs that you have intimacy anxiety.

Signs and symptoms of Intimacy Anxiety

Many psychologists suggest that for you to determine if you are suffering from intimacy anxiety is to look at your relationship history.

Doing so, you will be able to assess what happened to the relationship you had and you'll eventually know why it ended. You'll know why you are afraid of rejection or why you are afraid of losing your self-control thus making you fear getting intimate with another person. To help you determine which act to look for, here's a list of the signs of intimacy anxiety.

- Having the feeling that love is not for you and that you are not worthy of anyone's time, love, and affection

- Avoiding getting close with people because of the fear that you might be rejected when people see who you truly are

- Running away or sabotaging a developing relationship, especially when deeper feelings are starting to progress

- Reluctant in committing to a serious relationship due to avoidance of getting deeply hurt when the relationship ends

- Constantly testing your partner if they'll stick around or leave you, and even if you have proven that they will never leave, you are still insecure and feel the fear of losing them.

- Wearing an invisible mask in front of other people so you can please them instead of showing your real ski

- Always choosing the wrong person to have a relationship with even having the knowledge that the relationship is going nowhere

- Frequent breakups with partners or lovers

- Constantly indulging in dates but never allow others to get to know you deeper

Possible Root Causes of Fear of Intimacy

As discussed in the previous chapter, the fear of intimacy has been rooted from childhood. There are underlying issues that need to be addressed and experiences that have been kept but not confronted. Aside from the fear of rejection and engulfment, the items below are some other possible causes of developing intimacy anxiety.

1.   Being bullied during childhood

As what health experts say, bullying is serious and shouldn't be taken lightly. Fear of intimacy blossomed from either fear of being rejected or fear of engulfment; it can also blossom from both. Bullying can create a negative impact in someone's life. It makes those victims feel that there is something wrong with who they are and what they look. This results to a poor self-image and a negative perception. People who have bullied during their childhood days have the tendency of having this fear because they carry with them the hurt and rejection they felt from the past.

2.   Their parent's relationship

Your environment or surroundings greatly affect how you will grow. If you have witnessed your parent's relationship and found them be tumultuous your perception about intimacy, relationship and love is affected. There is a possibility that you'll develop a fear of intimacy if you've seen that the relationship of your parents isn't well. Many people make relationship-related decisions based on what they see from their own parent's relationship. If they see that their parent's relationship is happy, they want to have that kind of relationship in the future. But, if the relationship ended up with lots of pain and misery, some might think twice about committing in a relationship.

What can fear of intimacy do to your relationships?

Intimacy anxiety can destroy any relationship. The unwillingness to be open, having that great distrust, and refusing to commit to a relationship can inhibit the likelihood for a healthy intimacy.

The relationship may not ever have a chance to blossom because it is cut off even before the connection can occur. In some cases, the person with intimacy anxiety may opt for a partner who she or he believes as "safe" as a partner but not romantic or even sexually exciting. This trade off warrants that if rejection happens, it will not be as painful as a relationship involving romantic and sexual feelings.

On the other hand, there are people who will decide to have a series of meaningful and hollow sexual affairs minus the emotional closeness as another way to deal with their intimacy issues. This constant lack of fulfillment in several relationships may signal the need to assess yourself and see if there are any psychological explanations for never attaining genuine and true intimacy.

Chapter 4. Tips To Overcome Your Fear Of Intimacy

Before you even proceed to the tips presented below, it important to know that fear of intimacy is not a simple issue of self-distrust or poor self-image. Therefore, anyone who suspects that they are experiencing this intimacy phobia must not self-diagnose, as it is destructive and might worsen the whole issue. Go see a professional and allow yourself to be assessed. However, no matter how many years you've been struggling with bad relationships because of your intimacy anxiety, know that there are doable ways to overcome this fear.

The ways presented in this chapter are but simple tips that will help you deal with the feeling intimacy anxiety can bring to you. These tips can help you, somehow, to ease the negative feeling of being afraid of intimacy.

1. Commit to overcome the fear

It's always the first step to overcoming something: decision. Everything is your choice.

When you decide to move on with your life and live the life you deserve, you have to make a decision so you can make it happen. Everything starts with having that decision and being determined to really go with the change that you want to happen. If you are tired with having so many failed relationships or if you are afraid of running away from love, then it's time that you stand firm and resolve to put an end to it.

2. Write down your fears and try to understand them

The first step to winning a battle is knowing who you are battling against. This is also applicable in overcoming your fear of intimacy. Get a pen, think, and list down all the things that make you shy away from intimacy. Are you afraid of being betrayed? Rejection, perhaps? Anything that you think is contributing to your intimacy anxiety must be on that note. Perhaps you're afraid of getting close to anyone because you fear that they might just use you or hurt you in the end, write it down. Sometimes, the best way to face your fears is to know what they are and why you fear them.

3. Determine what you want in life

After you have written down your fears, ask yourself about the things you wanted in your life. Do you want to live happier? Do you want to be closer to your friends or family? Decide what you want and use this fact as a motivation to overcome your fear. Ask yourself a question, 'Do I want to live in fear?" if your answer is a big fat 'no', then you're good to go.

4. Just stop running away from people

If it means that you get out of your room and step out into the real world then go for it. It's time that you meet people and see them. It's time to get to know people again. Slowly, allow yourself to sincerely listen to what people have to say. You'll be surprise how amazing people are. You'll realize that when you stop running away from others, that's when you really know how beautiful they are despite of their ordinariness and weaknesses.

5. Accept that you are weak, so are others

One of the reasons why people are so afraid of intimacy is because they don't want others to see them in their most vulnerable state. Sometimes, people's egos are so big that they don't see their egos are already taking a toll on their happiness. Being weak is part of being human. You, your friends, and the people around you have their weak spots. Accept that fact and you'll live a life free of apprehensions. Release those inhibitions and repressions. Always remember that there is beauty in weakness. Being weak does not mean you are unacceptable. Those weaknesses make you human. Those things are the precious part of you. Those are the things that make you feel alive.

6. Loosen up

If you're far from being the titan named Atlas, stop being too serious like you're carrying the weight of the whole world. Life is short and your time in this earth will soon be gone, do not waste it by living in fear and being serious about all the things in life. Laugh more when you can. See the beauty of the world beyond its imperfections. While you still can, enjoy yourself. Your younger years will pass and you might not experience your youthful energy again. Don't try to be perfect because no one is, so why are you trying hard to be one?

7. Use affirmations; tell yourself that you deserve it

Relationship, love, trust, and affection are the results of intimacy. Opening yourself up for someone to see will result to trust and love. It will result to even deeper feelings and so much more. And one of the reasons why people have intimacy anxiety is thinking they don't deserve such great things. One of the main reasons why people are so afraid of committing is they don't think they deserve it. Once you end a relationship or lose someone, you might develop a mindset that maybe you don't deserve anyone in your life. These voices are the very reason why you won't have a relationship with someone else. If these things lurk inside your mind, just remember that everything happens for a reason. That you are subject to perfection and that you are allowed to commit mistakes. Tell yourself this every minute of every day.

8. Dare to trust again

Whether your trust issue is towards other people or for yourself, dare to fight it. Trusting someone might mean you're allowing them to betray you or hurt you but it will benefit you in the long run. Intimacy and trust go hand-in-hand. No one can achieve that level of intimacy without having that leap of faith and trusting that the person who'll see you will look at you without disgust.

9. Love yourself more

One last tip to help you overcome your intimacy anxiety is to beef up your self-confidence. Know that you are not perfect but your imperfection shouldn't be the reason why you should look down on yourself. Never think that you deserve less just because you think you'll never be enough for someone. Appreciate yourself more. Do things that would increase your self-confidence. Talk to yourself every morning and encourage yourself. Eat healthy foods, dress comfortably, and exercise. Meditate and know yourself better. Yes, love yourself more.

Conclusion

Thank you again for purchasing this book!

I hope this book was able to help you know more about fear of intimacy and tips on overcoming it.

Getting close to other people can be scary. It requires more from you that you never thought you have within you. However, no matter how scary you think it is, it isn't impossible regardless of what you've been through.

The next step is to develop yourself so you can be more comfortable with who you are. The issue with your self-image and how you see yourself play an important role in overcoming your fear of intimacy. If you're able make peace with yourself, then your fears will be easier to confront. Always, always know your worth. Never allow other people dictate who you should become or what you deserve. Because just any other human being in this world, you deserve every beautiful thing life can give you.

Know that it is never too late to start, so what are you waiting for? Deal with your fear of intimacy and live a happy life, free of fears.

Finally, if you enjoyed this book, then I'd like to ask you for a favor, would you be kind enough to leave a review for this book on Amazon? It'd be greatly appreciated!

Thank you and good luck!

Printed in Great Britain
by Amazon